HAL•LEONARD
INSTRUMENTAL
PLAY-ALONG

AUDIO
ACCESS
INCLUDED

PLAYBACK+
ed • Pitch • Balance • Loop

TROMBONE

PEACEFUL HYMNS

T0079345

Audio arrangements by Peter Deneff

To access audio visit:
www.halleonard.com/mylibrary
Enter Code
6827-3453-1777-8827

ISBN 978-1-70513-796-3

Visit Hal Leonard Online at
www.halleonard.com

Contact us:
Hal Leonard
7777 West Bluemound Road
Milwaukee, WI 53213
Email: info@halleonard.com

In Europe, contact:
Hal Leonard Europe Limited
42 Wigmore Street
Marylebone, London, W1U 2RN
Email: info@halleonardeurope.com

In Australia, contact:
Hal Leonard Australia Pty. Ltd.
4 Lentara Court
Cheltenham, Victoria, 3192 Australia
Email: info@halleonard.com.au

ABIDE WITH ME

TROMBONE

Music by WILLIAM H. MONK

ALL CREATURES OF OUR GOD AND KING

TROMBONE

Music from *Geistliche Kirchengesang*

ALL HAIL THE POWER OF JESUS' NAME

TROMBONE

Music by OLIVER HOLDEN

ALL THROUGH THE NIGHT

TROMBONE

Welsh Folksong

AMAZING GRACE

TROMBONE

Traditional American Melody

BE THOU MY VISION

TROMBONE

Traditional Irish

BLESSED ASSURANCE

TROMBONE

Music by PHOEBE PALMER KNAPP

COME, THOU FOUNT OF EVERY BLESSING

TROMBONE

Music from John Wyeth's *Repository of Sacred Music*

FAIREST LORD JESUS

TROMBONE

Music from *Schlesische Volkslieder*

FOR THE BEAUTY OF THE EARTH

TROMBONE

Music by CONRAD KOCHER

GREAT IS THY FAITHFULNESS

TROMBONE

Music by WILLIAM M. RUNYAN

HOLY, HOLY, HOLY

Music by JOHN B. DYKES

TROMBONE

HOW FIRM A FOUNDATION

TROMBONE

Traditional music compiled by JOSEPH FUNK

I NEED THEE EVERY HOUR

TROMBONE

Music by ROBERT LOWRY

IT IS WELL WITH MY SOUL

TROMBONE

Music by PHILIP P. BLISS

JUST AS I AM

TROMBONE

Music by WILLIAM B. BRADBURY

THE KING OF LOVE MY SHEPHERD IS

TROMBONE

Traditional Irish Melody

LET ALL MORTAL FLESH KEEP SILENCE

TROMBONE

17th Century French Carol

MY FAITH LOOKS UP TO THEE

TROMBONE

Music by LOWELL MASON

NEARER, MY GOD, TO THEE

TROMBONE

Music by LOWELL MASON

WERE YOU THERE WHEN THEY CRUCIFIED MY LORD?

TROMBONE

Traditional

WHAT A FRIEND WE HAVE IN JESUS

TROMBONE

Music by CHARLES C. CONVERSE

WONDROUS LOVE

TROMBONE

Southern American Folk Hymn